MACHINES ★ AT WORK

BULLDOZERS

BY MARV ALINAS

THE CHILD'S WORLD® • MANKATO, MINNESOTA

The Child's World

Published in the United States of America by The Child's World®
1980 Lookout Drive • Mankato, MN 56003-1705
800-599-READ • www.childsworld.com

PHOTO CREDITS
© David Frazier/Corbis: 7
© David M. Budd Photography: 4, 11
© Geoff du Feu/Alamy: 16
© iStockphoto.com/David Touchtone: 3
© iStockphoto.com/Robert Pernell: cover, 2, 12
© iStockphoto.com/Olivier Lantzendörffer: 20
© Johnny Lye/BigStockPhoto.com: 8
© Justin Kase/Alamy: 19
© Olivier Le Queinec/BigStockPhoto.com: 15

ACKNOWLEDGMENTS
The Child's World®: Mary Berendes, Publishing Director;
Katherine Stevenson, Editor

The Design Lab: Design and Page Production

LIBRARY OF CONGRESS CATALOGING-IN-PUBLICATION DATA
Alinas, Marv.
    Bulldozers / by Marv Alinas.
        p. cm. — (Machines at work)
    Includes bibliographical references and index.
    ISBN 978-1-59296-947-0 (library bound: alk. paper)
    1. Bulldozers—Juvenile literature. I. Title. II. Series.
    TA735.A446 2007
    624.1'52–dc22   2007013398

⭐ Contents

This bulldozer is pushing dirt in Colorado.

★ What are bulldozers?

Bulldozers are powerful earth-moving machines. They flatten bumpy ground. They push huge piles of dirt and rock. They break up hard ground, too.

⭐ How are bulldozers used?

Bulldozers are used for many jobs. They help people build roads and buildings. They push trees and brush out of the way. They move dirt and rock where they are needed. They even move trash at city dumps.

This bulldozer is pushing trash at a city dump.

crawler
tracks

↓

You can see how this bulldozer rests on its crawler tracks. ⭐

⭐ What are the parts of a bulldozer?

The bulldozer's body holds a big **engine**. The engine provides power that makes the bulldozer go. The bulldozer sits on wide metal belts. These belts are called **crawler tracks**. The tracks help the bulldozer move over bumpy ground.

9

★ The front of the bulldozer has a metal **blade**. The blade can be straight or curved. Metal arms move the blade up and down. The blade is used for pushing things. It is strong enough to push big piles of rock.

blade

This bulldozer's blade is slightly curved. It is pushing dirt and rock in Colorado.

ripper

When not in use, a bulldozer's ripper claws are kept up. How many claws does this bulldozer's ripper have?

Many bulldozers have **rippers** on the back. These rippers have big metal claws. They help bulldozers break up rocky or hard ground. Some rippers have two or three claws.

13

★ Who drives a bulldozer?

The bulldozer's driver is called the **operator**. The operator sits in the **cab**. The cab has a seat and **controls**. The operator uses the controls to make the bulldozer move. The controls make the blade go up and down. They make the ripper go up and down, too.

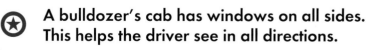

A bulldozer's cab has windows on all sides. This helps the driver see in all directions.

This bulldozer's crawler tracks are zooming through the mud.

★ How do bulldozers move?

A bulldozer crawls along on its moving metal tracks. The tracks can move forward or backward. They grip the ground. They also spread the bulldozer's weight. They keep the bulldozer from sinking in soft ground.

17

★ Bulldozers move slowly. They often go only about 6 miles (10 km) an hour. They are too slow and heavy to drive on streets. Trucks carry them from job to job.

This bulldozer is heading for a building site in England.

This huge bulldozer
is pushing coal.

⭐ Are bulldozers important?

People use bulldozers all over the world. They use them for all kinds of earthmoving jobs. Without bulldozers, these jobs would be hard to do. Bulldozers are very important!

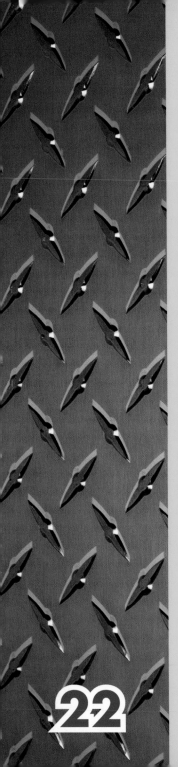

⭐ Glossary

blade (BLAYD) A blade is a part that is broad, flat, and usually thin. A bulldozer's blade pushes things.

cab (KAB) A machine's cab is the area where the driver sits.

controls (kun-TROHLZ) Controls are parts that people use to run a machine.

crawler tracks (KRAW-lur TRAX) Crawler tracks are metal belts that some machines use for moving.

engine (EN-jun) An engine is a machine that makes something move.

operator (AH-pur-ay-tur) A machine's operator is the person who runs the machine.

rippers (RIH-purz) On bulldozers, rippers are strong metal parts with claws. The claws loosen hard dirt and rocks.

 # Books

Butterfield, Moira, Chris Lyon (illustrator), and Gary Biggin (illustrator). *Bulldozers*. New York: Dorling Kindersley, 1995.

Martin, M. T. *Bulldozers*. Minneapolis, MN: Bellwether Media, 2007.

Mezzanote, Jim. *Giant Bulldozers*. Milwaukee, WI: Gareth Stevens Publishing, 2006.

Parent, Nancy, Bill Alger (illustrator), and David Desforges (illustrator). *The Bulldozer*. New York: Scholastic, 2003.

Teitelbaum, Michael, and Uldis Klavins (illustrator). *If I Could Drive a Bulldozer!* New York: Scholastic, 2002.

 # Web Sites

Visit our Web page for lots of links about bulldozers:
http://www.childsworld.com/links
Note to parents, teachers, and librarians: We routinely check our Web links to make sure they're safe, active sites—so encourage your readers to check them out!

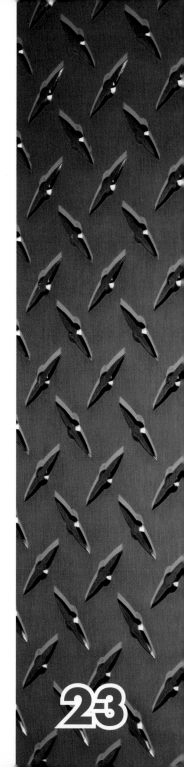

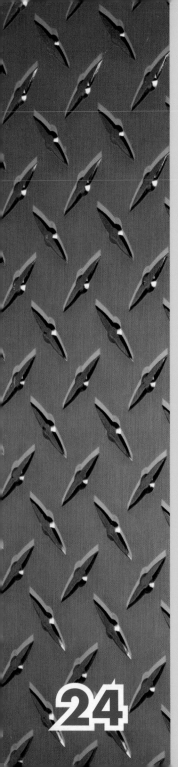

⭐ Index

⭐ About the Author

Marv Alinas has lived in Minnesota for over thirty years. When she's not reading or writing, Marv enjoys spending time with her dog and traveling to small river towns in northeastern Iowa and western Wisconsin.